Glimpsed in Pas.

Glimpsed in Passing

Poems

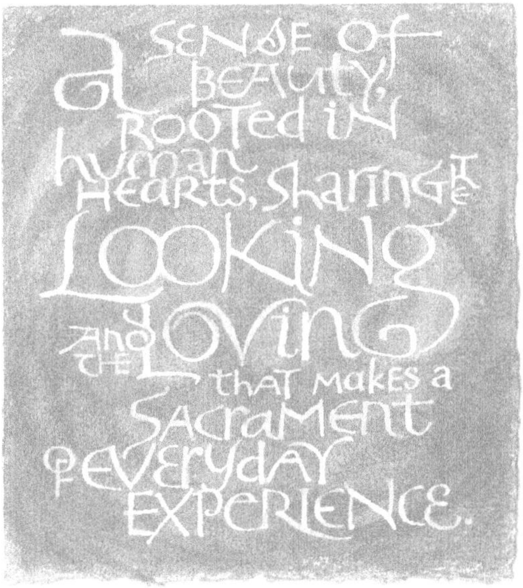
a sense of beauty, rooted in human hearts, sharing the looking and the loving that makes a sacrament of everyday experience.

JOY MEAD

wild goose publications
www.ionabooks.com

First published 2014 by
Wild Goose Publications, Fourth Floor, Savoy House,
140 Sauchiehall Street, Glasgow G2 3DH, UK,
the publishing division of the Iona Community.
Scottish Charity No. SC003794. Limited Company Reg. No. SC096243.

ISBN 978-1-84952-310-3

Overseas distribution
Australia: Willow Connection Pty Ltd, Unit 4A, 3–9 Kenneth Road,
Manly Vale, NSW 2093
New Zealand: Pleroma, Higginson Street, Otane 4170, Central Hawkes Bay
Canada: Bayard Distribution, 10 Lower Spadina Ave., Suite 400, Toronto,
Ontario M5V 2Z

Printed by Bell & Bain, Thornliebank, Glasgow

FSC www.fsc.org
MIX
Paper from responsible sources
FSC® C007785

Contents

Glimpsed in passing …

Not hours, days, years … not even minutes … but moments: maybe when the sun lightens the stones of an old wall, when you notice the sparkle of drops of rain on a flower, wonder at the beginning-of-the-world green of the unfurling beech leaf – these are precious jewels of moments glimpsed in passing, held for a short time, then let go into the bigger picture that is life in all its fullness. The letting go matters, the moving on matters and so does expression, amid the pain and sorrow of the world, of the beauty of the glimpsed moment. That is what life at its best consists of – its poetry. It gives life's moments their importance. It's what we'll remember …

The opposite of a boat adrift (p45) has something to do with what we glimpse in passing and everything to do with resurrection, living in each moment, living more than …

Joy Mead
April 2014

Making paths

(For Frances)

We work among your trees,
talking as our hands
touch earth and wood.
Spirit, it seems to me,
enters the world
through the wildness
of words, rooted yet branching
unconfined, disobedient
to garden rules, digressing
into the diversity
of conversation.

What we plant usually outwits us
and will surely outlive us, growing
gently over our attempts
to make a way
through the woods.

Grassy glades offer pauses
like the silence of night
in a forest of changing
perceptions.

We, the makers and the talkers,
create the remembered way
by walking the path home.

Tonight …

… we tread lightly,
our way softened by the setting sun.
Deer stand silently in a far field
their distance aristocratic, almost sacred;
waiting, sustained, like us, by the glory
of a red light that bleeds upwards
from an unseen horizon.

They return to the trees:
take the way into the dark
on light but not ignorant feet.
They know we are here.
We know where they live.
That shared knowledge
gives the moment power
to bestow blessings.

Gentle awakening

Sun-warmed, colour-filled stones:
the old wall holding back the wind
is lightened by lichen
and the day's promise.
The pause created
by the garden door
is an invitation
to open the mind
and leave it open.

The known but always surprising
walk into the garden
is fragrant with love,
half-forgotten hopes
and half-remembered stories.
Butterflies and bees are undisturbed
by our brief presence.
Thoughts beyond tears stay close
to small lives and forms.

Those who tend growing things
must believe in the resurrection
of the dead seed; understand
what it is that outgrows
our dreams, our little lives.

Childhood's ungathered flowers
will continue to grow without fading
or losing their sweet smell.
Joy is morning bright,
Memory is lovely
and knows that it is lovely.

Christening at Candlemas

(For Louisa)

There is something about winter bareness
that brings all life to essentials
and the comfort of light hoarded
in littleness.

When Adam and Eve left the Garden of Eden,
so the story goes, they were comforted
by an angel who turned snowflakes
into snowdrops: small light in dark times
like candles blessed between winter solstice
and spring equinox, then carried to each room
to make perhaps the year's first poem.

So, in the promise of earliest spring,
when courage and faith are necessary
we might offer on your special day
snowdrops, candlelight and the touch of water:
small signs of our trust in your future,
suggestions of glory beyond our knowing,
not bound to our dreams but shining
in the wonder that is your young life
and the blessing of our unmade tomorrows.

Today we give you the name
chosen for you: Louisa
to make you part of the story,
to bless the child you are
and, not ours to choose,
the woman you will become:
a self you will not find
but create as you live.

Illumination

In the Abbey Church
on a wild October evening
power cut and a small peace:
the perfect light
of hundreds of candles,
quiet guttering of flame,
fire of memory,
fire at the heart
of our being,
caressing the dark
honouring it

Rainbows appear day
on day, more enigmatic
than the shouting stones.

Beneath a fig tree *

(For Eva, to celebrate the Bread Festival
at Schumacher College where there are fig trees)

Leaves edged with sunlight –
the clothes of Eden;

the space beneath welcoming
the thinker. This one my own
fig tree for the moment.

Birds above me – hidden
by a thick cover of leaves –
are sounds only

and mingle with the distant voices
of children playing on a green.

I can see, through an arch
in the stone wall, a light and airy space
set for all as an eating place
and Eva carries bread
for the Festival:
bread of sorrow
bread of joy,
to the table set for sharing
a meal and a beginning.

* Nathanael under the fig tree: John 1:48.
Living in peace 'under his own fig tree' – 1 Kings 4:25 and Micah 4:4

Song of the trees

(Life is a phenomenon of the second generation of stars, from *Biochemistry,* Christopher Mathews and K.E. van Holde)

Stories older than memory, longer than history,
gift that is rooted and whispering above,
stars in the trees, holding their mystery:
trembling creation, dancing in love.

> *Oak is for kingship; birch for fertility;*
> *Hazel for wisdom; rowan for mystery;*
> *Pine for nobility; hawthorn for death;*
> *Holly for immortality.*

Sensations of prayer, music of our minds,
waves from the past, half-remembered sounds,
stardust and earthdust, promise on the winds,
wisdom for life where beauty astounds.

> *Oak is for kingship; birch for fertility;*
> *Hazel for wisdom; rowan for mystery;*
> *Pine for nobility; hawthorn for death;*
> *Holly for immortality.*

Hope in all that has lived and is living,
seen in our frailty and moment of birth,
glitter of star become rooted, life-giving
known in the depths of our mothering earth.

Oak is for kingship; birch for fertility;
Hazel for wisdom; rowan for mystery;
Pine for nobility; hawthorn for death;
Holly for immortality.

Today …

… I'll try to make peace
in practice and poetry.
I'll choose words and images carefully,
avoiding all that proscribes, restricts,
oppresses, destroys, humiliates,
patronises, demonises or enslaves.

I'll try to use words
that open minds,
widen moral vision
and motivate the will;
words that show an alternative
to famine, war, racism,
torture and violence,
unjust structures, systems
and relationships.

I may talk about sex
or about violence
but I will resist the media urge
to conflate the two.

I'll not abandon reason
but I'll ask questions
that challenge the relentless
course of logic.

I'll value imagination, story
and poetry that show
there is another way.
I'll fight no fights, not even 'good' ones.
I'll not stand up for Jesus
    or be a soldier of anything
    not even the cross;
    nor wave any flaming swords;
I'll address no one as Lord
    or mighty conqueror
    or put on any sort of armour
    not even the armour of Christ
    or the dressings of power.
I'll not march for Jesus
    or anyone else.
I'll parade no nationalistic flags,
    nor bang any triumphalist drums.

I'll be a pilgrim
and try to walk lightly
for the sake of the earth,
and the diversity of life
it sustains.

I'll recognise the fragility
and finite nature of the earth
our only home and resist creatively

all that denies fullness of life by:
playing, laughing and dancing
planting trees and sowing seeds
making and sharing bread
... and ice cream!
lighting candles,
being alive to song and symbol.

I'll look more
and listen more.
I'll live more moments
as given moments.
I'll make this day,
and every day,
a holy day.

I shall make mistakes
and admit to them humbly.

Today I'll dream –
of all sorts of people together,
loving, sharing, playing, dancing
celebrating difference.

And at the end of the day
when things are much the same
I'll continue to hope.
I'll remember that the personal
is always political; that inner peace
cannot be separated from wholeness

and health in community;
that small acts of beauty
by small groups of people
still carry the potential
to change the world.

Wool, wood, stone, Ardalanish beach

(for Jan)

The windswept beach
where we collect wood
is loud with possibilities.

Cloudshaped woolmakers
float on the hills.
Row on row they work
on the intricate patterns
of landscape.

A rock with the presence
of a Ronald Rae sculpture
is a wind-worn, sea-washed
testament, loud
in its silence.

The evening will be filled
with warm dreams
and the wood-fire whispering
of household gods.

A grey day

Uncertain of the future but free
to allow the sorrows and joys
of lost experience to be reclaimed
and redeemed with words
as yet unborn, I see what must be said
illuminated by its own light only.

In the joy of connections
I come to know
the power of hope
which is beyond my perception
of happiness.

Abiding

(For Kathy on her retirement as Leader of the Iona Community)

Abiding ...
... is unshakeable
but full of surprises,
steadfast and earth-centred
but holy becoming,
a way of staying mindful
with memories:

a rainbow day on the island,
bridges of blessings everywhere,
a rolled out cloth of light
and the Abbey church full
of many-coloured words;

the whisper of candles
soft enough for the possibility
of angels and poetry
to illuminate the manuscript
of our minds;

the silence of stones and deeps
and wonders; the sea spleenwort
that continues to grow, to thrive
on the south wall;
the peace of time and place
we know remarkably well;

songs in the Camas kitchen
and the music of blessing
that fills the Abbey, falls
on us, then rests in the air,
moving towards silence.
like the ring of a rock
when it's tapped
with a stone;

the isle full of the noise
of many conversations:
stories to live by, told
on the hills, and by the sea,
the thoughts, words, actions
of our lives that exist
for a moment
so always have being
like the wind
that carries sounds
far over the sea;

the soul that recognises
itself as living water;

taste on the tongue, grain
in the mouth, bread broken

shared, a place at the table,
bread between us;
a quiet meeting of minds
that knows wholeness
in a Gandhian spinning wheel
and a voluptuous woman
offering flowers and fruit.

Abiding ...
... is the nature of shepherds,
some friends, parents,
and trusted leaders.
It's a gentle way
of being, more faith-full
than keeping watch
and gives to all things
a local habitation
and a name.

In a world of unlikeness
I will offer this likely
and almost lost word
to celebrate your presence,
your gifts and gifting
which are, for me
and for this Community,
abiding.

* And there were in the same country shepherds abiding in the field … (Luke 2:8)
I've always loved the word 'abiding' particularly in this line in the Authorised Version. What a pity 'abiding' doesn't appear in newer translations!

Conkers

Seeds whose time has come
showered earthwards, outburst
their armoured shells,
each one with power to be
no more, no less
than total tree.

Some I gathered that day
for memory's sake
I feel in my pocket now
wizened, their gloss
left in hidden places,
their being neither transformed
nor yet unchanging.

Theirs is not to become
life in its flesh
but to token in some art form
life's rich mesh
and to be a suggestion
of resurrection.

Alone …

… in a cloud-darkened churchyard
I sit unnaturally still, wanting
the almost unbearable to be changed

into something tolerable.
There's no consolation
in reason, mind fails

to ease the turbulence
which is quiet only
in connections, in the closeness
of trees and butterflies,
birds and grass,
and in the wonder of knowing
as the sun breaks through:
all life is here
and it is good.

Christmas

I wish for you these gifts
of Christmas time:

light of heavenly star
and earthly candle;
flicker of firelight
that is winter warmth
and speaks friendship;

music of angel voices
blessing the earth;
music of human voices
singing their dreams;

pine and holly berry,
colours of winter's emotions;
cinnamon and orange,
the scents of memory;

freshly baked bread to share
with friend and stranger;

the hallowed darkness
and the enduring wonder
of what we know
and what we cannot know;

questions around a crib
in the faraway stable
of our imagination
where a tiny light
continues to shine
and the story goes on;

the touch and breath
of our being alive
in moments of pure joy
that are all we need
of meaning;

hands reaching out
across years and differences
in uncertain hope.

Red paintchart poem

Windsor Red, Letter Box,
Celebration,
Garnet Symphony,
Blazer, Book Room,
Moroccan Velvet,

Picture Gallery
Rectory Red

Rustic Red, Fox,
Red Earth

Eating Room, Roasted Red,
Rich Burgundy.

Ruby Fountain

Red earth

Clay
Terracotta
Brick
Roan
Rust
Coral
Ruby

Sugar pink
Scarlet
Vermilion
Tomato
Dragon's blood
Mahogany
Raven

Big words

(for Steve)

Write the words big
then you'll begin to see
their hidden life,
what it means
to shape letterforms,
and make memory lovely,
to reveal possibilities beyond
naming, to understand maybe
the shapes and colours,
the little bits of imagery
that might touch meaning,
to see the way all things belong
to all other things.

Small writing, small talk
may fill up silence with nothing
but a word will always be more than
itself – like a hand held out
in the darkness, or the movement
of a moment that becomes the way
the earth turns.

Write the words big
you told me, release them
while they still have energy.
and something
will happen.

A photograph of birdsong?

(For Anne, who planted the thought)

Isn't it always blue? When I see the sky
and carpets of bluebells, don't they sound
like birds in spring, woods come alive?

Is it ever possible to take a silent photograph
of the woods in the first breath of warm air?
When the call of this year's first cuckoo
echoed across the fields at Easter
wasn't that the sound of fresh leaves
against blue, and the nutty scent
of awakening beech trees.

To make a poem

learn to swim without water,
or fly on the ground:
it's all make-believe.

Walk on water:
not an element for walking
unless you trust
imagination.

Walk on air – sometimes.
Say 'Yes' to the moment.

But the hard task
will always be
to walk lightly
on your own element:
the good earth.

Skeleton of a poem

Bare trees
against a darkening sky,
brachial.

Driftwood, death white
discarded bones
from unknown shores.

Prayer

Breathe in, and become
a part of all I see.
Inspire, witness and feel,
wordless or word-filled
thought-led or thought-free,
that it is good.

Breathe out in cold air.
See breath, hear heartbeat.
Seek no meaning but to be present
in this once and for all moment;
to breathe and see wholeness in
dew on spiders' webs,
mist that lies in the valley
and trees that reach through
as if connecting to the earth's
life-breath and mine;

to feel my heart beat
alive, awake, whole;

to take in the endless unknowable
and know the rhythm of ordinariness
to be the form of prayer ...

April 2006

(For Fred when he was first diagnosed with Alzheimer's, with love)

April, Eliot's cruellest month*:
the air heady with promise.

Beech leaves unfurl
and the blue
of bluebells is the deepest
of mysteries in the quiet
of the moment.

Frail things that live
and once lived,
yesterdays lost in the mist,
tomorrows that may not be,
gather in a dreamlike web.

So I think of you, dear friend
and cells that die
taking with them
words that shape
images of the past
and pictures of the future.

What is now beyond telling
is written on your skin,
hidden deep in your eyes,
carried on every hair of your head.

You gather light
sufficient for today

like the flowers I saw once
locked in a cage
early in the morning
on a railway platform.

* See T.S. Eliot's *The Waste Land*

October 2009

(In memory of Fred Kaan and for all his family and friends)

The cage is open.
The spirit is free.
All the flowers
of a life well lived
with strength and gentleness:

the sound of your voice
and the words from your pen,
the magic of your smile
and the tears that tell stories
more loudly than words,
the way you confront evil
and your anger at injustice,
jazz and apples,
wine and good bread,
your gifts and giftedness,
your enabling friendship,
your intensity and love of life,
the way you listen
with mindfulness
and celebrate the ordinary,
your deep faith in the goodness
at the heart of all things

have been put into our hands,
that we may truly sing
resurrection
and rejoice in the life
of one pilgrim
who has found the path
home.

The gate …

… fills a gap in a fence
that may one day be a hedge.
One side is home,
the other the whole world.
The gate is a stepping off place
that keeps little in or out.
Badgers come under.
Squirrels come over.
Rabbits are rare visitors
and I've yet to see a deer
come near the gate.

Wind and water easily
breach its defences.
It doesn't divide or control
but joins cut and garden grass
with wild and wind-waving seedheads:
green to green
earth to earth.
dust to dust …

The smell of summer grass
isn't confined to any one side
of a gate that is but an interruption
in the air like the threshold
from life to death.

Glimpsed in passing …

What is the opposite
of a boat adrift … ?

It's the way it's always been:
to reach the sea, to stand
watching, waiting; to know
that nothing can be unravelled
to its core

but is like reflecting
where wild flowers
gathered in a vase, framed
by a shore cottage window
make of themselves
a sea-wide subject:
the beauty
of things together.

A blackbird sings
and the song echoes
in fragments of memory.

A choir, unison
of sound,
and a thought
in the wind
the music
of non-oppression.

The first daffodil opens
in the way daffodils do
each spring: fragile
expected, known.

Cuckoo returning:
a joy in the tragedy
of the world

What awaits us
on the other side
of silence
might be an ecstasy
of free-flowing movement
melted and released
by a flame
we learn to see
burning in every bush.

Hold the seed gently.
Know you are holding
a field of wheat,
a loaf of bread,
food with friends,
the joy of sharing.

A story re-told:
Five thousand fed on a hillside
and a memory resurrected:
power cut darkness
on the road before dawn

candles in a window,
porridge and coffee,
a warm fire and friendship.

A sense of beauty, rooted
in human hearts, sharing
the looking and the loving
that makes a sacrament
of everyday experience.

Resurrection is living
more than ...

To imagine …

… a time in the boat,
rowing close to the safety
of the shore yet aware of its distance,
reveals the need to pause,
to rest the oars on my knees.
Not to look down
but out to the far horizon,
up to the sky, to be still
and remain one small part
of the bigger picture.

Unknowing

The oystercatcher's cry
is a rumour
we don't understand
and never will;

while the corncrake mocks
from a place in the grass
we think we know
but never find.

These things live
without our mapping
their being or knowing
their meaning. It seems
they will always
find us.

Written in water

Words meeting and linking,
twisting and turning,
moving, always moving;
a whispering,
a waterfall,
an echoing splash,

a yearning to form
an understanding
of life in letters,
to shape a perfect image
in words.

Who am I?

I can only deny
what colludes
to limit my space
by being
as fully human
as I can,
welcoming
in each moment
the unlooked-for
joy.

It's good you know
and who's to say
I won't succeed.

I do not know God

but I do know:
  wind in the treetops
  and the sound of the sea
  as it reaches the shore;
I do know:
  the loveliness of laughter,
  the smell of a baby's head,
  the trust in a child's touch,
  the light in an old woman's eyes,
  hope in a kiss.
I do know:
  music coming from
  and leading to
  silence;
  words on a page -
  story and poetry
  connecting heart and mind,
  thought and imagination.
I do know:
  the mystery of colour
  in an artist's palette
  and the way the potter's hands
  shape the clay.

I do not know God
but I do know:

leaf mould and lichen,
wood rot and fungi,
new shoots and unfurling leaves,
soil and soul,
death and renewal;
I do know:
ripening wheat,
rising dough,
and sharing bread;

I do not know God
but I do know:
worms, bees and butterflies,
pattern, change and movement,
fragility and vulnerability;
I do know:
the surprise of strawberries,
the wonder of apples,
and that there is beauty
in a cancer cell magnified.
I do know:
morning sunlight
as it touches
each blade of grass;
the flicker of the smallest flame
and the furthest star.

I do not know God
but I do know:
  the kindness
  of cleaners and wisdom
  in unexpected places;
I do know:
  that energy and love,
  vision and discernment
  make possibilities
  endless.
I do know:
  suffering and joy,
  darkness and light
  as integral to being
  fully alive.

I do not know God
but I do know
  that the teachings of Jesus
  are being lived out,
  if not by the church,
  then by grassroots movements
  everywhere.
I do know
  of small groups of people
  making and mending,
  working and wondering,
  growing and sharing,
  meeting and striving,

questioning and protesting,
living and loving
together.

I do not know God
but I do know:
that the intensity of love
can be creative
or destructive.
I do know:
that defining goodness
is difficult, if not impossible
but we know a good person
when we meet one.

I do not know God
but I do know
that beauty is gratuitous
and peace, beyond certainty
or purpose, is in the knowing
the unknowing.

A time to walk … and a time to stand …

(For Jan)

Blackberries in a borrowed milk can,
driftwood collected in a Co-op bag,
elderberries and mushrooms,
hazelnuts and sloes,
hips and crabapples.

All the world
was once wild like this
and life for looking,
seeing and gathering
the fruits of moments:
the bird in the tree,
the morning light,
the first daffodil,
spring blowing through
the ruins of winter,
the smell of summer grass,
children's laughter,
an apple and a tree
in Milton's garden,
the do-not-disturb wonder
of our knowing
time is nothing
but the running down
of clock weights

and the swing
of the pendulum.

Speed is violence.

Go home slowly carrying your excuses
for being where you have been!

Dandelions …

… gold without affectation
the poor person's beauty

like the language that Tyndale sought
everyday, here, everywhere
and wanted to offer
to ordinary people
as what life at its best
consists of

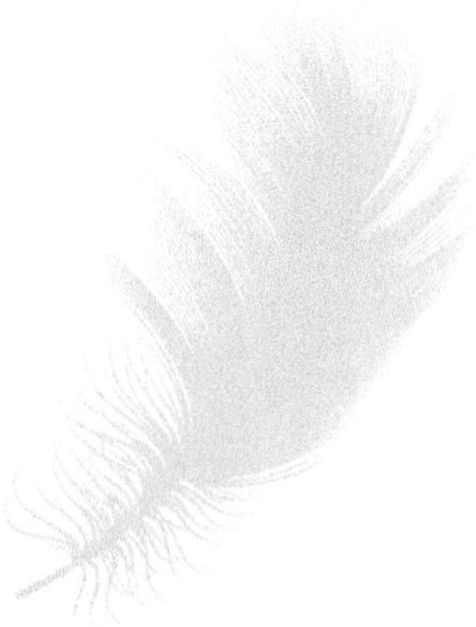

Thanksgiving for Columba *

Columba of
the rocks and roots and rolling waves,
rain-drenched earth, changing skies and empty horizons,
coming home and moving on.

Columba of
the music of wind and seabird cries,
the poetry of wild geese and lowing cattle,
the vision of sharing bread and stories.

Columba
Man of solitude and simplicity,
community and compassion,
Soul friend.

We celebrate with gratitude and hope
your being and your openness
to the blessedness of all things.

Columba who saw the blessing of beauty
and Iona as a light for all times:

with you
we weep
for depths of poverty
and pinnacles of wealth;
for hostility, impersonality,
suffering, indifference
and all that harms people
and all living things

with you
we laugh
for humanity's raucous energy
and generosity of spirit
for angels, clowns, smiling faces
and all that heals people.

We celebrate with gratitude and hope
your being and your openness
to the blessedness of all things.

Because of imagination, legend and prayer
because of love and grace
no act is inconsequential
and no story without significance.
In our knowing and unknowing;
in the quiet space held within
that is Columba's vision and forever Iona,
we hold memories, remembrance,
and the whisperings
of a people's pride.
We hold out for others
the poet's bread
and the people's poetry.

We celebrate with gratitude and hope
the holiness of being
and the blessedness of all things

* Written for the Service of Thanksgiving and Commitment on the 75th Anniversary of the founding of the Iona Community held at Govan Old Parish Church on 9th June, 2013

On the earth

(For Anne)

When you're on dry soil
and the rain comes
and the scent
is as if it runs
from the veins of the gods
don't look up
to the sky
for the miracle.
Look at your feet
at the earth
you walk on.
From there are springing
nothing but miracles:
the roots, the beginnings,
the little flowers
that are what life
at its best consists of.

Smell and look and know
Wonder in the silence
at paradise unspoken
for it's this wonder
that makes you
a human being
fully alive.

Note: There is a word for rain on the dry earth: *petrichor* derived from petra- /stone and –ichor / the fluid that flows in the veins of the gods in Greek mythology.

'Models of mind'*

A small thing, outside my sense
of size or reason;
not meaning but relationship
to all things, a prehistoric memo,
formed by an artist's hands
to a model of mind,
a familiar maybe
of massive and distant
standing stones.

Silent,
yet full of the sound of land
of wind and waves,
song and story.
Lament or joy,
beginning or ending
now or then
or when?

A form full of questions.
it asks to be held
to display its relationship
to all the things of our lives
as a preserved violin
might ask to be played.

Its solid 'yes'
is the song
of blackbird,
or ascending lark,
the spaciousness in music,
a condition of the heart,
true to our shared earth.

* An exhibition of fascinating work by Jim Pattison (at the Pier Art Gallery, Stromness, Orkney in 2013) based on the carved stone balls from the islands of Scotland.

A workaday fiddle …

… a modest instrument
tough enough to travel
the Arctic silence in a kayak
and well suited to an owner*
who knew where to learn
the secrets of survival.

Black paint almost worn away
by fingers low down
in the fiddling position –

tells a story of Scottish reels
in the cold, cold air
of remote trading posts;

tells of dancing feet;
tells as clearly
as a worn floor;

tells about the people's longing
for curlew calls, oystercatcher cries
and the songs of home.

Silent, behind museum glass
it holds its story,
keeps its memory magic,
waits to speak of home
to wanderers everywhere;

waits for the heart of one man's
almost forgotten story
to be heard again
in the people's music.

* Arctic explorer John Rae. His fiddle, recently restored by Mark Shiner and played by Jennifer Wrigley, is displayed in Stromness Museum.

Apple tree

by a wall, alone,
a stranger to itself,
forgotten,
without the companions
of an orchard,
fruiting
to feed butterflies
and our trust
that earth will provide

Not magic, but
earth rooted
and good.

Peace

is the many-coloured
bird of dawning
flying over
our disillusion
and despair;
the rainbow hope
of what tomorrow
might become.

Seeds

hold their own story,
a subtle wisdom
that grows
at nature's pace.

To save seeds
is to hold a thing
of beauty;
a sacred act.
To plant seeds
is to believe
in tomorrow,
an act of faith
and source
of enlightenment

A farm without seeds
is like a house without light

Steps

(For Ruth – Iona 1997)

When you live on an island
everything happens
somewhere else, they say.
These small dancing steps
on the sand
to the rhythm of sea
and music of wind
are a story waiting to begin
in another place.

Now, a long way
inland,
I can't pick out
the steps you taught us
then, or bring to mind
the name of the dance
the four of us did,
on the beach.
But I remember the pattern,
the weaving and threading
the shape and sharing
of a turning point.
I remember hands held out
and hands clasped;
I remember, against a greying sky,
dancing
into the sun again.

Steps 2

(North End, Iona, 2011 – for Jan and in memory of Ruth and Isabel)

The weaving and threading,
the shaping and sharing:
a pattern that has stayed
with me since that day
in 1997 when four of us,
danced on the beach
to the steps you showed us.

Today there will be no visible dance;
no abandoned joy for the two of us left,
just the to and fro, in and out
of the rhythm of this day
as we walk the remembered space.
Nothing is said, nothing is done
but we know that hands reach out
from the past, leading us
on to try new steps,
explore new patterns,
to go on dancing the story
into our own uncertain future.

'The sea wants to be visited'*

Shall we go down to the shore today,
down the path where grass is sweet,
and follow the light to the edge of the bay
past the mill and its chattering stream.

Shall we go down to the shore today,
with our windblown thoughts of waving wheat,
and follow the scents of seaweed and salt
down to where earth and water meet.

Shall we go down to the shore today,
to the place of dreams and ghosts of bread,
to savour the moment and stand at the edge
where time is early and all has been said.

* Gaelic proverb

Beads

When the thread breaks
the beads scatter,
to far corners
with a loud voice:
a hailstorm of change,
demanding attention.

I hold on to the thread
as we retrieve each bead.
Then one by one I touch them
differently threaded and know
all is changed but there is hope
in connection restored.

One thing only is needful
to know end and beginning
as one and make the circle
whole.

Seeking

Rhyme the colours.
Play with the light.
Carry the words
into the dark.
The perfect poem
waits to be written.
The words out there
somewhere in the light
ask to be drawn in
wrapped around, arranged
to make a defence
against the dark:
a fully formed poem –
the story of a life.

'A few … may creep back, silent'*

and so he did, my granddad,
back to his wife
and six young daughters,
carrying inside his untold story.

Home and silent,

a man gassed and damaged:
a useless arm, his mind
not quite as it should be
and a fondness for drink.

Home and silent,

they lived with his story
this broken man,
who once made shoes
for a living, then went
reluctantly to war,
and the woman who nurtured
his silence and bore him
another girl, a child with a mind
not quite as it should be.

The words that tell are lost
like those of another story:

my great-uncle who deserted,
was given shelter once,

and never heard of again –

lost in the great silence.

But the energy, the life
and the loving,
stronger than the killing
and the wounding,
bigger than words,
is here in my living,
honouring the silence,
bearing on the body
what I cannot know
and only poetry can tell.

* Wilfred Owen, from *The Send Off*

Prayer 2

as the poetry of the quiet people
who may not inherit the earth,
ever
but do it less harm
than some;

who are the essential colours
in the painting of life,

do as they have to
every working day
to ease with their care
our ordinary lives:

to bring the milk
and fill the forms,
to dig the ground
and do the sums,
to ice the cakes
and cut the hair,
to serve the food
wash the clothes,

to record the deaths
and births and marriages
and bury the dead,

to touch each life with care,
gently
as if each one matters
individually,

as they do.

Re-reading Middlemarch at 70

50 years married and
re-reading Middlemarch

Remembering the book,
the story, the experiences of first reading

An old copy, Penguin, brown at the edges,
smelling of ageing

Now the humour and the pathos is different,
looking back, not forward

Like turning over part of my life
Experiencing each part differently

To have grown old in love.
For love to grow

How different now
Dorothea's vision
that was once my own
or more or less
See now the value of the ordinary
the everyday beauty of life
in all its detail and wonder

Moving books

Ordering and arranging shelves
cleaning and caring
shifting memories like dust,
holding each book tenderly
holding in my heart
the one who wrote
and the one who gave,
who shared the wonder
of words, knowing each of us
is made of poetry, story and place,
remembering a daughter's passion
for Jane Austen and a hillside
of reading on a sun-filled day
when she was just beginning
and I was learning to let go,
revisiting moments
and holding the books
that have made me.

Silence

It’s life-giving, to know stillness
in sacred moments savoured
each time as if the first time:
the play of light
on the surface of water,
the hen harrier’s soundless gliding
between us and the open sea,
the fullness of the seed
resting in my hand,
the particular quiet
when music pauses,
that special, transforming second
when a child’s wide-awake gaze
is covered in sleep and I watch.

Wordless moments
when everything is stilled
and held life-long in love
and silence.

Flowers of thought

A morning in December
– almost Christmas –
and a jug filled
with pieces of sunlight:
a gift of early daffodils.
They lighten the room
with a suggestion of spring,
outsplendour the fairy lights,
yellow the air with hope,
and bring all things
to this moment,
like the brimstone butterflies,
who all summer flew the fields
also full of promise.

One day in summer
(For Kathy, Lesley and Sally)

Faith
might be
four almost wise women
talking of sex
and bringing up boys,
around a tombstone
in the churchyard
of Govan Old Church
in Glasgow
on a hot day
in June.

Hope
almost certainly is.

Abiding (2)

(Bedouin shepherds driven off ancestral lands by Israeli Defence Force)

If shepherds no longer abide
what will happen to hope,
to the promise of Christmas?
What will happen to the stories
if ordinary people
are no longer able to live
as their spirit leads them.

We all carry some connection
to the story and the stillness,
the waiting in fields,
on hillsides, in homes,
in churches and monasteries.
Suffering prevails
when there is no imagination
and the story remains untold.

If shepherds are driven from their lands
and are no longer abiding, it matters to us.
What happens to one
happens to us all
and in the injustice
we all lose something
of what it means
to be human.

Curlew skull

Wafer of bone,
image of stillness,
all soft tissue and feathers
gone, no smell, no colour,
but a sense of something
basic and essential
resting on my hand.
Fragile, yet surviving
the storms of winter.
Silent, yet evoking
the always surprising call
heard in the silk of the wind
on an Orkney shore.
The music of the isles
recalled in a moment
between sea and sky,
in memories unrealised
until this intense looking.

Out of the woods

Do we now talk of heart
when we tell of trees?
Once there was a spirit
in the woods, now
what we hear
is the lonely sound
of wind and rain.

All winter I've wondered
at the naked beauty
of storm-battered trees.
I see form and patterning
similar to our human hearts:
our small and smaller arteries
our vital trunks and branches
unseen, unless an artist imagines
or a photographer reveals,
for life or beauty's sake.

And as the trees
will leaf in summer,
we know our over-worked
and sometimes broken hearts
will beat our quiet hope
and be whole again.

Bread poetry

Late summer sunlight
on the floor of the forest:
dead wood, fungus, damp earth,
yeast – this is where we make
our bread and shape
our words.

Bread is the form
of my poem:
seed, flour, dough
in my hand
shape and expression,
the rhythm of the loaf.

Bread broken: taste
on my tongue,
grain in my mouth –
the poetry of my being:
beauty of all
our beginnings
earth, food, word.

Pancakes and gooseberry jam

We bottle words in wonder,
preserve them in a way
that nourishes imagination
and holds moments of sweetness
against the world's sorrows.

Words for today:
small things, small times:
the colours of a day in May,
new leaves, first flowers,
and butterflies,
the sound of a hunting kite,
the scents of cow parsley
and early summer grass.

Then those pancakes
with gooseberry jam
that we ate in the sun:
food for today,
taste on the tongue,
in the mind,
in the heart
words for tomorrow,
words to re-create
and re-member,
that keep hope alive
and sustain a friendship.

Golden Wedding

13th June, 2014

Knowing
the everyday beauty
of fifty years
of days
in all their detail
and wonder,
knowing
that love is so much more
than when we stood diffident
in the church porch
on our Wedding Day
wanting what was good,
not knowing
what it was –
until now.

The road home

... seems shorter now,
steeper, with more stones,
noisier in places
but mostly silent,
darker sometimes
yet the light at the end
is often very close.
There is still the search –
but not now for meaning
but for beauty.
There are exquisite moments
in unexpected places –
to be old is to see clearer
the loveliness of things.

The end is around a bend
I can't yet see
but it's there
waiting for me
and you
to be ready.

One day, I'll turn that bend
alone and, I hope,
content.

… in the detail

The diamond drops of rain
on Lady's Mantle leaves
are held by tiny hairs.

A feather
in Henry Moore's garden
is caught in the sunlight,
ephemeral,
against the weight
of human existence.

Butterflies fill the summer air
and two red admirals stay late
to feast on apples left to rot.

Skeleton leaves
are trodden underfoot
and winter pods
reveal through lace
tiny expectant seeds.

A mind that mourns
the worms that drown
knows these close-by
epiphanies, knows space
between things, always open,
uncertain, inconclusive,
moves in the universality
of details beyond sight-seeing,
thrives on small things ...

Note

Making paths and *Prayer 2* first appeared in *A Way of Knowing*, Joy Mead, Wild Goose Publications, 2012.

Acknowledgements

As always, my thanks to everyone at Wild Goose Publications and especially to Sandra for encouragement and for the kindly, conscientious and efficient way she handles the writing and the writer. Thank-you too to Stephen Raw (StephenRaw.com), also for his encouragement and especially for the beautiful cover artwork.

About the author

Joy Mead is a member of the Iona Community and the author of *The One Loaf*, *Making Peace in Practice and Poetry*, *Where are the Altars?*, *Words and Wonderings* and *A Way of Knowing*, all published by Wild Goose Publications. She has been involved in development education and justice and peace work and occasionally leads creative writing groups.

Wild Goose Publications is part of the Iona Community:

- An ecumenical movement of men and women from different walks of life and different traditions in the Christian church
- Committed to the gospel of Jesus Christ, and to following where that leads, even into the unknown
- Engaged together, and with people of goodwill across the world, in acting, reflecting and praying for justice, peace and the integrity of creation
- Convinced that the inclusive community we seek must be embodied in the community we practise

Together with our staff, we are responsible for:

- Our islands residential centres of Iona Abbey, the MacLeod Centre on Iona, and Camas Adventure Centre on the Ross of Mull

and in Glasgow:

- The administration of the Community
- Our work with young people
- Our publishing house, Wild Goose Publications
- Our association in the revitalising of worship with the Wild Goose Resource Group

The Iona Community was founded in Glasgow in 1938 by George MacLeod, minister, visionary and prophetic witness for peace, in the context of the poverty and despair of the Depression. Its original task of rebuilding the monastic ruins of Iona Abbey became a sign of hopeful rebuilding of community in Scotland and beyond. Today, we are about 250 Members, mostly in Britain, and 1500 Associate Members, with 1400 Friends worldwide. Together and apart, 'we follow the light we have, and pray for more light'.

For information on the Iona Community contact:
The Iona Community, Fourth Floor, Savoy House, 140 Sauchiehall Street, Glasgow G2 3DH, UK. Phone: 0141 332 6343
e-mail: admin@iona.org.uk; web: www.iona.org.uk

For enquiries about visiting Iona, please contact:
Iona Abbey, Isle of Iona, Argyll PA76 6SN, UK. Phone: 01681 700404
e-mail: ionacomm@iona.org.uk